HAL•LEONARD®

SAXOPHONE
PLAY-ALONG

AUDIO
ACCESS
INCLUDED

PLAYBACK+
Speed • Pitch • Balance • Loop

# Jazz icons

## Play 8 Songs with Notation and Sound-alike Audio

INCLUDES PARTS FOR
B♭ AND E♭ SAXOPHONES

## CONTENTS

T0081611

To access audio visit:
**www.halleonard.com/mylibrary**

Enter Code
1753-7806-4321-7057

Musicians:
Saxophone – Jason Weber
Trumpet – Jamie Breiwick
Drums – Devin Drobka
Bass – John Christensen
Piano – Mark Davis

Produced by Chris Kringel
Mixed by Kyle White

ISBN 978-1-4950-7716-6

HAL•LEONARD®

7777 W. BLUEMOUND RD. P.O. BOX 13819 MILWAUKEE, WI 53213

For all works contained herein:
Unauthorized copying, arranging, adapting, recording, Internet posting, public performance,
or other distribution of the printed or recorded music in this publication is an infringement of copyright.
Infringers are liable under the law.

Visit Hal Leonard Online at
**www.halleonard.com**

# Body and Soul

**Words by Edward Heyman, Robert Sour and Frank Eyton**
**Music by John Green**

Copyright © 1930 Warner Bros. Inc.
Copyright renewed; extended term of Copyright deriving from Edward Heyman assigned and effective
January 1, 1987 to Range Road Music Inc. and Quartet Music
Extended term of Copyright deriving from John Green, Robert Sour and Frank Eyton assigned to Warner Bros. Inc. and Druropetal Music
All Rights for Quartet Music Administered by BMG Rights Management (US) LLC
International Copyright Secured   All Rights Reserved
Used by Permission

4

# Con Alma

By John "Dizzy" Gillespie

© 1956 (Renewed 1984) DIZLO MUSIC CORPORATION
All Rights Controlled and Administered by EMI APRIL MUSIC INC.
All Rights Reserved   International Copyright Secured   Used by Permission

Rhythm: Swing

# Speak No Evil

By Wayne Shorter

Copyright © 1965 Miyako Music and Milky Way Express, Inc.
Copyright Renewed
All Rights Administered by Songs Of Kobalt Music Publishing
All Rights Reserved   Used by Permission

# Take Five

By Paul Desmond

© 1960 (Renewed 1988) Desmond Music Company
All Rights outside the USA Controlled by Derry Music Company
International Copyright Secured   All Rights Reserved

# There Will Never Be Another You

Lyric by Mack Gordon
Music by Harry Warren

© 1942 (Renewed) MORLEY MUSIC CO., FOUR JAYS MUSIC PUBLISHING and MATTSAM MUSIC
All Rights Reserved

# Tune Up

**By Miles Davis**

Copyright © 1963 Prestige Music c/o The Bicycle Music Company
Copyright Renewed
International Copyright Secured  All Rights Reserved

# Work Song

By Nat Adderley

© 1960 (Renewed) by UPAM MUSIC CO., a division of Gopam Enterprises, Inc.
All Rights Reserved   Used by Permission

# Oleo

**By Sonny Rollins**

Copyright © 1963 Prestige Music c/o The Bicycle Music Company
Copyright Renewed
International Copyright Secured  All Rights Reserved

# Oleo

By Sonny Rollins

Copyright © 1963 Prestige Music c/o The Bicycle Music Company
Copyright Renewed
International Copyright Secured   All Rights Reserved

# Body and Soul

**Words by Edward Heyman, Robert Sour and Frank Eyton**
**Music by John Green**

Copyright © 1930 Warner Bros. Inc.
Copyright renewed; extended term of Copyright deriving from Edward Heyman assigned and effective
January 1, 1987 to Range Road Music Inc. and Quartet Music
Extended term of Copyright deriving from John Green, Robert Sour and Frank Eyton assigned to Warner Bros. Inc. and Druropetal Music
All Rights for Quartet Music Administered by BMG Rights Management (US) LLC
International Copyright Secured   All Rights Reserved
Used by Permission

**Cadenza**
**Rubato**

# Con Alma

By John "Dizzy" Gillespie

© 1956 (Renewed 1984) DIZLO MUSIC CORPORATION
All Rights Controlled and Administered by EMI APRIL MUSIC INC.
All Rights Reserved   International Copyright Secured   Used by Permission

# Speak No Evil

By Wayne Shorter

Copyright © 1965 Miyako Music and Milky Way Express, Inc.
Copyright Renewed
All Rights Administered by Songs Of Kobalt Music Publishing
All Rights Reserved   Used by Permission

# Take Five

**By Paul Desmond**

© 1960 (Renewed 1988) Desmond Music Company
All Rights outside the USA Controlled by Derry Music Company
International Copyright Secured   All Rights Reserved

# There Will Never Be Another You

Lyric by Mack Gordon
Music by Harry Warren

© 1942 (Renewed) MORLEY MUSIC CO., FOUR JAYS MUSIC PUBLISHING and MATTSAM MUSIC
All Rights Reserved

# Tune Up

By Miles Davis

Copyright © 1963 Prestige Music c/o The Bicycle Music Company
Copyright Renewed
International Copyright Secured   All Rights Reserved

# Work Song

By Nat Adderley

© 1960 (Renewed) by UPAM MUSIC CO., a division of Gopam Enterprises, Inc.
All Rights Reserved  Used by Permission

# HAL•LEONARD® SAXOPHONE PLAY-ALONG

The Saxophone Play-Along Series will help you play your favorite songs quickly and easily. Just follow the music, listen to the audio to hear how the saxophone should sound, and then play along using the separate backing tracks. Each song is printed twice in the book: once for alto and once for tenor saxes. The melody and lyrics are also included. The online audio is available for streaming or download using the unique code printed inside the book, and it includes **PLAYBACK+** options such as looping and tempo adjustments.

## 1. ROCK 'N' ROLL

Bony Moronie • Charlie Brown • Hand Clappin' • Honky Tonk (Parts 1 & 2) • I'm Walkin' • Lucille (You Won't Do Your Daddy's Will) • See You Later, Alligator • Shake, Rattle and Roll.
00113137 Book/Online Audio ....................................... $16.99

## 2. R&B

Cleo's Mood • I Got a Woman • Pick up the Pieces • Respect • Shot Gun • Soul Finger • Soul Serenade • Unchain My Heart.
00113177 Book/Online Audio ....................................... $16.99

## 3. CLASSIC ROCK

Baker Street • Deacon Blues • The Heart of Rock and Roll • Jazzman • Smooth Operator • Turn the Page • Who Can It Be Now? • Young Americans.
00113429 Book/Online Audio ....................................... $16.99

## 4. SAX CLASSICS

Boulevard of Broken Dreams • Harlem Nocturne • Night Train • Peter Gunn • The Pink Panther • St. Thomas • Tequila • Yakety Sax.
00114393 Book/Online Audio. ....................................... $16.99

## 5. CHARLIE PARKER

Billie's Bounce (Bill's Bounce) • Confirmation • Dewey Square • Donna Lee • Now's the Time • Ornithology • Scrapple from the Apple • Yardbird Suite.
00118286 Book/Online Audio....................................... $16.99

## 6. DAVE KOZ

All I See Is You • Can't Let You Go (The Sha La Song) • Emily • Honey-Dipped • Know You by Heart • Put the Top Down • Together Again • You Make Me Smile.
00118292 Book/Online Audio ....................................... $16.99

## 7. GROVER WASHINGTON, JR.

East River Drive • Just the Two of Us • Let It Flow • Make Me a Memory (Sad Samba) • Mr. Magic • Take Five • Take Me There • Winelight.
00118293 Book/Online Audio ....................................... $16.99

## 8. DAVID SANBORN

Anything You Want • Bang Bang • Chicago Song • Comin' Home Baby • The Dream • Hideaway • Slam • Straight to the Heart.
00125694 Book/Online Audio ....................................... $16.99

## 9. CHRISTMAS

The Christmas Song (Chestnuts Roasting on an Open Fire) • Christmas Time Is Here • Count Your Blessings Instead of Sheep • Do You Hear What I Hear • Have Yourself a Merry Little Christmas • The Little Drummer Boy • White Christmas • Winter Wonderland.
00148170 Book/Online Audio ....................................... $16.99

## 10. JOHN COLTRANE

Blue Train (Blue Trane) • Body and Soul • Central Park West • Cousin Mary • Giant Steps • Like Sonny (Simple Like) • My Favorite Things • Naima (Niema).
00193333 Book/Online Audio ....................................... $16.99

## 11. JAZZ ICONS

Body and Soul • Con Alma • Oleo • Speak No Evil • Take Five • There Will Never Be Another You • Tune Up • Work Song.
00199296 Book/Online Audio ....................................... $16.99

# ♭ HAL•LEONARD®

Visit Hal Leonard online at **www.halleonard.com**

*Prices, contents, and availability subject to change without notice.* 0417